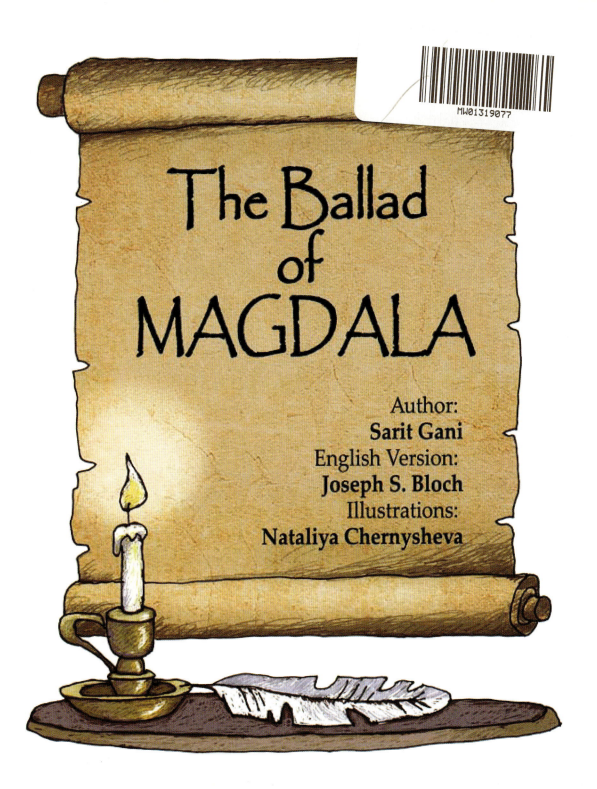

The Ballad of MAGDALA

Author:
Sarit Gani
English Version:
Joseph S. Bloch
Illustrations:
Nataliya Chernysheva

It was but a few years ago
I bet it was not many.
A call came forth from far Mexico
A vision sweeter than any.

A pilgrims' guesthouse to build
A nice, pleasant place to be.
In the Holy Land, where Jesus walked,
On the shores of the Galilee Sea.

An early morn of spring it was,
Green garments the fields all wore.
When workers, young and sturdy ones,
Headed to Magdala's shore.

Hard at work, digging the foundation
Hands steady, backs firm to adore.
Alas, first strike the pick went down
And met a stubborn floor.

Wiping away the dirt,
Unto their eyes amazed,
A mosaic floor and wall paintings
At a bench of stone they gazed.

With every bin of dirt removed,
They realized and watched agog,
The bench and the mosaic floor
 Were not but part of a synagogue.

With a room for all to study,
And one for all to pray
And a library for the scrolls.
Homes, warehouses, fishmongers' stores,
Ritual baths and bowls.

Stone by stone revealed to the world,
After centuries interred.
Buried not so deep, less than a meter down.
They called: "Come dig us up!" but no one heard…

But the jewel of all was a stone block,
On which a Menorah was engraved.
A seven-branched candelabrum
I bet it was not eight.

Hence, the mason must have seen it
At the Temple in Jesus' days.
And carried this memory dearly
From Jerusalem to Galilee Bay.

Imagine a bunch of small boats,
Small boats in the water so blue.
Tanned fishermen heave and haul
The brimming nets they threw.

On the shore, long rows
Of salted fish dry in the sun's view.
This industry is Magdala's pride,
The best you ever knew.

Here come a-bouncing fair maidens
On their way to the synagogue's school.
Young Mary, she is with them,
A flower among the few.

No notebooks or textbooks
To bring by the armloads.
With parchment and quill
They skip down the hill.

Mary – a girl, a teenager, a woman grown –
Hears Jesus' words of worth.
"Blessed are the meek", he says,
"They will inherit the earth."

She follows him to Jerusalem;
Two other women take part,
In finding his empty tomb,
For a new life to start.

Now years had come and gone
Two thousand, to be exact.
When ancient Magdala was unearthed
This was God's will and act.

The news spread quite fast
And they hastened and rushed
From all over the world to see:
Archeologists, historians and clergymen
To the shores of the Galilee.

All gathered around the spot
And affirmed the discovery's worth:
From all that we know, from Jesus' time,
This synagogue is the oldest on earth.

Good news to Jerusalem came
Good news at fair Rome arrived:
There has been a great miracle
On the shores of the sea
And History's come alive.

 And who was the one to give Magdala
His Apostolic blessing?
Why it was Pope Benedict XVI, The Holy Father,
To Magdala addressing.

Yes, something loftier than a guesthouse
Must have been in God's plan to be
For Magdala, the fishermen's town,
On the Sea of Galilee.

Copyright© 2017 Intelecty Ltd.

All rights reserved. No part of this book may be used or reproduced by any means, graphic, electronic or mechanical, including photocopying, recording, taping or by any information storage retrieval system without written permission of the publisher except in the case of brief quotations embodied in critical articles and reviews.

ISBN: 978-965-7607-43-5

Intelecty Ltd. Publishing House

76 Hagalil St.

Nofit 36001

Israel

Tel: +97249930922

Fax: +972722830147

galit@gestelit.co.il

Printed in the Holy Land

JesusBooks4Kids

Printed by GESTELIT
info@gestelit.co.il

More in the series:
History Comes Alive in the Holy Land

 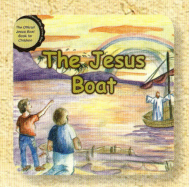 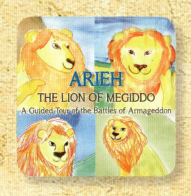

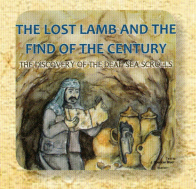 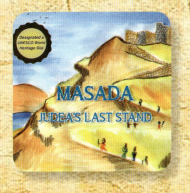

Magdala

Although Magdala is mentioned several times in the scriptures (Maria Magdalena is a prominent clue), it came as a huge surprise in the year 2009, when remains of an ancient fishery town were revealed near the contemporary settlement of Migdal, on the western shores of the Sea of Galilee. All this happened while digging foundations for a pilgrims' guesthouse on the shore.

Right at the start, the workers unearthed a first century synagogue - one of only seven synagogues from this period in the world. It is more than likely, that Jesus himself had taught here on His ministry in the Galilee. Along with the synagogue, there was discovered an entire first century city, with homes and warehouses, stores and ritual bathes. Most exciting was the discovery of a stone block, on which a Menorah shape was engraved. It tells that the artist must have seen the original Menorah in Jerusalem before 70 AD (year of the Temple's destruction).

After this stirring discovery, there was erected on site a one-of-its-kind Chapel, the 'Duc In Altum'. With a view of the Sea of Galilee and a unique boat-shaped altar, this chapel commemorates Jesus preaching from the boat. 'Duc In Altum' draws its name from Luke 5:4 where Jesus instructs Simon Peter to "launch into the deep". On May 26, 2014, during his pastoral pilgrimage to the Holy Land, Pope Francis blessed the tabernacle, which resides on the altar in the Boat Chapel.

'Duc In Altum' also exalts the presence of women in the Gospel, first and foremost Mary from Magdala, who was a follower of Jesus and one of the three who found His empty grave.

In just a few short years, with only part of the site excavated, Magdala has already become a very special place of history and culture, as it provides an authentic location to walk and pray where Jesus taught, and to connect with the first century life of Jesus' followers.